Dedication

To all those who ever struggled with learning a
foreign language and to Wolfgang Karfunkel

Also by Yatir Nitzany

Conversational Portuguese Quick and Easy

....

Conversational French Quick and Easy

....

Conversational Spanish Quick and Easy

....

Conversational German Quick and Easy

....

Conversational Russian Quick and Easy

....

Conversational Polish Quick and Easy

....

Conversational Hebrew Quick and Easy

....

Conversational Yiddish Quick and Easy

....

Conversational Arabic Quick and Easy
Classical Arabic

....

Conversational Arabic Quick and Easy
Lebanese Dialect

....

Conversational Arabic Quick and Easy
Palestinian Dialect

....

Conversational Arabic Quick and Easy
Egyptian Dialect

....

Conversational Arabic Quick and Easy
Jordanian Dialect

....

Conversational Arabic Quick and Easy
Emirati Dialect

....

Conversational Arabic Quick and Easy
Syrian Dialect

Conversational
Italian
Quick and Easy

YATIR NITZANY

Printed in the United States of America

Foreword

About Myself

For many years I struggled to learn Spanish, and I still knew no more than about twenty words. Consequently, I was extremely frustrated. One day I stumbled upon this method as I was playing around with word combinations. Suddenly, I came to the realization that every language has a certain core group of words that are most commonly used and, simply by learning them, one could gain the ability to engage in quick and easy conversational Spanish.

I discovered which words those were, and I narrowed them down to three hundred and fifty that, once memorized, one could connect and create one's own sentences. The variations were and are *infinite*! By using this incredibly simple technique, I could converse at a proficient level and speak Spanish. Within a week, I astonished my Spanish-speaking friends with my newfound ability. The next semester I registered at my university for a Spanish language course, and I applied the same principles I had learned in that class (grammar, additional vocabulary, future and past tense, etc.) to those three hundred and fifty words I already had memorized, and immediately I felt as if I had grown wings and learned how to fly.

At the end of the semester, we took a class trip to San José, Costa Rica. I was like a fish in water, while the rest of my classmates were floundering and still struggling to converse. Throughout the following months, I again applied the same principle to other languages—French, Portuguese, Italian, and Arabic, all of which I now speak proficiently, thanks to this very simple technique.

This method is by far the fastest way to master quick and easy conversational language skills. There is no other technique that compares to my concept. It is effective, it worked for me, and it will work for you. Be consistent with my program, and you too will succeed the way I and many, many others have.

Contents

INTRODUCTION TO
THE PROGRAM

People often dream about learning a foreign language, but usually they never do it. Some feel that they just won't be able to do it while others believe that they don't have the time. Whatever your reason is, it's time to set that aside. With my new method, you will have enough time, and you will not fail. You will actually learn how to speak the fundamentals of the language—fluently in as little as a few days. Of course, you won't speak perfect Italian at first, but you will certainly gain significant proficiency. For example, if you travel to Italy, you will almost effortlessly be able engage in basic conversational communication with the locals in the present tense and you will no longer be intimidated by culture shock. It's time to relax. Learning a language is a valuable skill that connects people of multiple cultures around the world—and you now have the tools to join them.

How does my method work? I have taken twenty-seven of the most commonly used languages in the world and distilled from them the three hundred and fifty most frequently used words in any language. This process took three years of observation and research, and during that time, I determined which words I felt were most important for this method of basic conversational communication. In that time, I chose these words in such a way that they were structurally interrelated and that, when combined, form sentences. Thus, once you succeed in memorizing these words, you will be able to combine these words and form your own sentences. The words are spread over twenty pages. In fact, there are just nine basic words that will effectively build bridges, enabling you to speak in an understandable manner understandable manner (please see Building Bridges on page 38). The words will also combine easily in sentences, for example, enabling you to ask simple questions, make basic statements, and obtain a rudimentary understanding of others' communications. I have also created Memorization Made Easy techniques for this program in order to help with the memorization of the vocabulary (please see page 12). Please also see page 13, Reading and Pronunciation of the Italian Language, prior to starting this program.

My book is mainly intended for basic present tense vocal communication, meaning anyone can easily use it to "get by" linguistically while visiting a foreign country without learning the entire language. With practice, you will be 100 percent understandable to native speakers, which is your aim. One disclaimer: this is not a grammar book, though it does address minute and essential grammar rules (please keep your eyes peeled for grammar footnotes at the bottom of each and every page of the program). Therefore, understanding sentences with complex obscure words in Italian is beyond the scope of this book.

People who have tried this method have been successful, and by the time you finish this book, you will understand and be understood in basic conversational Italian. This is the best basis to learn not only the Italian language but any language. This is an entirely revolutionary, no-fail concept, and your ability to combine the pieces of the "language puzzle" together will come with great ease, especially if you use this program prior to beginning an Italian language class.

This is the best program that was ever designed to teach the reader how to become conversational. Other conversational programs will only teach you phrases. But this is the only program that will teach you how to create your own sentences for the purpose of becoming conversational.

THE ITALIAN LANGUAGE

The official language of Italy and it has evolved over time, primarily because of the poet Dante Alighieri, who modernized the language by blending the Italian dialects, Sicilian and Tuscan. While the language's Tuscan roots are more prevalent, the now-extinct language, Dalmatian, also inspired Dante. With the combination of these three Romance dialects, the Italian language evolved into its modern state. Spoken by approximately seventy million people, Italian shares the title with Latin as co-official language of the Vatican City, as Italian has Latin roots. Though the language is most widely spoken in Italy, Italian is also spoken in some areas of Switzerland, Croatia, France, Slovenia, and Albania.

Spoken in: Italy

MEMORIZATION MADE EASY

There is no doubt the three hundred and fifty words in my program are the required essentials in order to engage in quick and easy basic conversation in any foreign language. However, some people may experience difficulty in the memorization. For this reason, I created Memorization Made Easy. This memorization technique will make this program so simple and fun that it's unbelievable! I have spread the words over the following twenty pages. Each page contains a vocabulary table of ten to fifteen words. Below every vocabulary box, sentences are composed from the words on the page that you have just studied. This aids greatly in memorization. Once you succeed in memorizing the first page, then proceed to the second page. Upon completion of the second page, go back to the first and review. Then proceed to the third page. After memorizing the third, go back to the first and second and repeat. And so on. As you continue, begin to combine words and create your own sentences in your head. Every time you proceed to the following page, you will notice words from the previous pages will be present in those simple sentences as well, because repetition is one of the most crucial aspects in learning any foreign language. Upon completion of your twenty pages, *congratulations*, you have absorbed the required words and gained a basic, quick-and-easy proficiency and you should now be able to create your own sentences and say anything you wish in the Italian language. This is a crash course in conversational Italian, and it works!

For further assistance in the memorization and pronunciation of the vocabulary of this program, you may also purchase the audio version of this book, which is featured on Amazon, Audible, and iTunes.

Reading and Pronunciation in Italian

Ce - pronounced as "che."
Ci - pronounced as "chi."

When *ci* is followed by a vowel then the *i* drops.

Cia	- pronounced as	"cha."	
Cie	- pronounced as	"che."	
Cio	- pronounced as	"cho."	

Ciu - pronounced as "chu."

Ch - pronounced as "k."
Chi - pronounced as "ki."
Che - pronounced as "ke."
Chi - pronounced as "ki."

Ge - pronounced as "je."
Gi - pronounced as "ji."

When *gi* is followed by a vowel then the *i* drops.
Gia - pronounced as "ja."

Gie - pronounced as "je."
Gio - pronounced as "jo."
Giu - pronounced as "ju."

Gh - before *e* or *i* the *h* drops (*laghi* / "lakes" pronounced as "lagi").
Gli - pronounced as the *lli* in "millions", the *g* is silent.
"I want" / *voglio* - pronounced as "vol-yo."
figlio / "son" - pronounced as "fil-yo."
Gn - the *g* drops and the *n* is pronounced as "ny" (lasagna).

Sce - and *sci* pronounced as "sh."
Sch - before *e* or *i* pronounced as "sk."
When *sci* is followed by a vowel the *i* is dropped.
Scia - pronounced as "sha."

Scie - pronounced as "she."
Scio - pronounced as "sho."
Sciu - pronounced as "shu."

In Italian, when *s* is followed by a vowel and is the second or third or further syllable of the sentence, then it's pronounced as a "z."
Casa is pronounced as "caza."

Z is pronounced as "ts" or "tz."

—It's also important to note that in Italian, whenever encountering double consonants, each letter must be pronounced. *Pizza* is pronounced as "piz-za." Nonna is pronounced as "non-na."

NOTE TO THE READER

The purpose of this book is merely to enable you to communicate in Italian. In the program itself (pages 16-40) you may notice that the composition of some of those sentences might sound rather clumsy. This is intentional. These sentences were formulated in a specific way to serve two purposes: to facilitate the easy memorization of the vocabulary and to teach you how to combine the words in order to form your own sentences for quick and easy communication, rather than making complete literal sense in the English language. So keep in mind that this is not a phrase book!

As the title suggests, the sole purpose of this program is for conversational use only. It is based on the mirror translation technique. These sentences, as well as the translations are not incorrect, just a little clumsy. Latin languages, Semitic languages, and Anglo-Germanic languages, as well as a few others, are compatible with the mirror translation technique.

Many users say that this method surpasses any other known language learning technique that is currently out there on the market. Just stick with the program and you will achieve wonders!

Again, I wish to stress this program is by no means, shape, or form a phrase book! The sole purpose of this book is to give you a fundamental platform to enable you to connect certain words to become conversational. Please also read the "Introduction" and the "About Me" section prior to commencing the program.

In order to succeed with my method, please start on the very first page of the program and fully master one page at a time prior to proceeding to the next. Otherwise, you will overwhelm yourself and fail. Please do not skip pages, nor start from the middle of the book.

It is a myth that certain people are born with the talent to learn a language, and this book disproves that myth. With this method, anyone can learn a foreign language as long as he or she follows these explicit directions:

* Memorize the vocabulary on each page

* Follow that memorization by using a notecard to cover the words you have just memorized and test yourself.

* Then read the sentences following that are created from the vocabulary bank that you just mastered.

* Once fully memorized, give yourself the green light to proceed to the next page.

Again, if you proceed to the following page without mastering the previous, you are guaranteed to gain nothing from this book. If you follow the prescribed steps, you will realize just how effective and simplistic this method is.

THE PROGRAM

Let's Begin! "Vocabulary"
(Memorize the Vocabulary)

I	I am	Io	Io sono
With you	Con te, con lei / **(Plural)** con voi
With him / with her	Con lui / con lei
With us	Con noi
For you	Per te, per lei / **(Plural)** per voi
Without him	Senza lui
Without them	Senza loro
Always	Sempre
Was	Era
This	Questo
Is	(verb) è / (conjunction) si
Sometimes	A volte / qualche volta
You	(Informal)Te, tu/(formal)Lei/(P)Voi
Are you / you are	**(Temporary)** sei, **(permanent)** siete
Better	Meglio
Today	Oggi
He / She	Lui / Lei
From	Da, di, dall / dalla

Sentences from the vocabulary (now you can speak the sentences and connect the words)

I am with you

Io sono con te

This is for you

Questo è per te

I am from Italy

Sono dall'Italia

Are you from Milan?

Sei di Milano?

Sometimes you are with us at the mall

A volte siete con noi al centro commerciale

I am always with her

Io sono sempre con lei

Are you without them today?

Sei senza di loro oggi?

Sometimes I am with him

A volte io sono con lui

*In Italian, the preposition "from" could be either *da* or *di*. Depending on the case, though, it could be a bit confusing.
*In Italian, the pronoun "you," *te* is the informal and lei is the formal. *Voi* is plural.

I was	Ero
To be	Essere
The	Lo, il, l', gli, i, la, le
Same	Stesso
Good	(**Male**) Buono / (**fem**) buona
Here	Qui
It's / it is	è
And	E
Between	Tra
Now	Adesso / ora
Later / After	Più tardi, dopo
If	Se
Yes	Sì
Then	Allora / dopo / poi
Tomorrow	Domani
Very	(**M**) Molto / (**F**) molta
Also / too / as well	Anche

Between now and later
Tra adesso e dopo
If it's later, then it is better tomorrow
Se è tardi, allora è meglio domani
This is good as well
Questo è anche buono
Yes, you are very good
Sì, sei molto bravo
I was here with them
Ero qui con loro
You and I
Io e te
The same day
Lo stesso giorno

*In Italian the article "the" has a few different tenses.

-*Lo* — masculine words that start with *gn, pn, ps, x, y, z* (and *s* plus a consonant)

-*Il*—used for any other (masculine) words beginning with consonants, except for *gn, pn, ps, x, y, z* (and s plus a consonant).

-*L'*—before a vowel or an *h*

-*Gli* —plural form of *lo*

-*I* —the plural form of *il*

-*La* — feminine form

-*Le* —plural form of *la*. Plural remains *le* even if the following word is an *h* or a vowel.

17

Me	Me
Ok	Ok
Even if	Anche se
Afterwards	Dopo
Worse	Peggio
Where	Dove
Everything	Tutto
Somewhere	De qualche parte
What	Che cosa?
Almost	Quasi /pressapoco
There	Là, lì
Maybe	Forse

Afterwards is worse
Dopo è peggio
Even if I go now
Anche se vado ora
Where is everything?
Dove è tutto?
Maybe somewhere
Forse da qualche parte
What? I am almost there
Che cosa? Sono quasi Là
Where are you?
Dove sei?

*In Italian, pronouns have different tenses.
- "My"—*mio* (male), *mia* (female), *miei* (male plural), *mie* (female plural)
- "Your" (informal)—*tuo* (male), *tua* (female), *tuoi* (m. plural), *tue* (f. plural)
- "Your" (formal)—*vostro* (male), *vostra* (female), *vostri* (m. plural), *vostre* (f. plural)
- "His"/"Her"—suo (male), sua (female), suoi (m. plural), *sue* (f. plural)
- "Our"—*nostro* (male), *nostra* (female), *nostri* (m. plural), *nostre* (f. plural)
- "Their"—*il loro* (male), *la loro* (female), *i loro* (m. plural), *le loro* (f. plural)

House	Casa
In	In
Car	Automobile / macchina
Already	Già
Good morning	Buongiorno
How are you?	Come stai?
Where are you from?	Di dove sei?
But / however	Ma
Hello	Ciao
What is your name?	Come ti chiami?
How old are you?	Quanti anni hai?
Son	Figlio
Daughter	Figlia
At	A
A	(M) uno, un / (F) una
Hard	(*Hard object*) Duro / (*difficult*) difficile
Still	Ancora
Your	Tuo / tua

She is without a car, so maybe she is still at the house?
Lei è senza una macchina, allora forse lei è ancora a casa?
I am in the car already with your son and your daughter
Sono in macchina già con tuo figlio e tua figlia
Good morning, how are you today?
Buon giorno, come stai oggi?
Hello, what is your name?
Ciao, come ti chiami?
How old are you?
Quanti anni hai?
This is very hard, but it's not impossible
Questo è molto difficile, ma non è impossibile
Where are you from?
Di dove sei?

*In Italian, the article "a" has three different tenses.
- Male–*uno* (*gn, j, pn, ps, s* plus consonant, *x, y, z*)
- *Un*—for any other words
- Female–*una*
- *Un'*—before all vowels or *h*—*un'orologio* "a clock"
- Keep in mind *uno* doesn't have this rule concerning vowels and *h*.

Thank you	Grazie
For	Per
Everything	Tutto
This is	Questo è
Time	Ora
But	Ma
No / Not	No
I am not	Io non sono
Away	Lontano
That	(M) questo (F) questa (N) questo
Similar	Simile
Other / Another	Altro
Side	Lato
Until	Fino a
Yesterday	Ieri
Without us	Senza noi
Since	Da
Day	Giorno
Before	Prima

Thanks for everything
Grazie per tutto
It's almost time
E 'quasi ora
I am not here, I am away
Io non sono qui, io sono lontano
That is a similar house
Questa è una casa simile
I am from the other side
Io sono dall'altro lato
But I was here until late yesterday
Ma io ero qui fino a tardi ieri
Since the other day
Dall'altro giorno

*In Italian, *ora* is time, *volte* means (how many) times, and tempo is (length of) time.
*In Italian, the prepositions "of" and "from" could be *di* or *da*. When preceding the article "the," each of these (*di* and *da*) become prefixes and form one character.
di+il=del, di+lo=dello, di+l'=dell', di+la=della, di+i=dei, di+gli=degli, di+le=delle
da +il=dal, da+lo=dallo, da+l'=dall', da+la=dalla, da+i=dai, da+gli=dagli, da+le=dale

I say / I am saying	Dico
What time is it?	Che ora è?
I want	Voglio
Without you	Senza te
Everywhere /wherever	Ovunque / dovunque
I go / I am going	Vado
With	Con
My	(Sing M/F) Mio/mia (Plu) miei
Cousin	(M)Cugino(MP)cugini/(F)cugina(FP)cugine
I need	Ho bisogno
Right now	Adesso / ora
Night	Notte
To see	Vedere
Light	Luce
Outside	Fuori / esterna / esterno
That is	Questo è
Any	Qualsiasi
I see / I am seeing	Vedo

I am saying no / I say no
Dico no / io dico no
I want to see this during the day
Voglio vedere questo durante il giorno
I see this everywhere
Vedo questo ovunque
I am happy without any of my cousins here
Sono felice, senza nessuno dei miei cugini qui
I need to be there at night
Ho bisogno di essere lì durante la notte
I see light outside
Vedo la luce fuori
What time is it right now?
Che ora è adesso?

*In Italian, you aren't required to place a personal pronoun preceding a conjugated verb. For example, "I am saying no" is *dico no*. The word "I" (io) before a conjugated verb isn't required. For example, *io voglio sapere la data* / "I want to know the date" can be said *voglio sapere la data* since *voglio* already means "I want" in the conjugated form, although saying *io* isn't incorrect! The same rule applies to *tu/lui/lei/loro/noi/vostro*—they aren't required to be placed prior to the conjugated verb, but if they are, then it isn't wrong. There are a few exceptions, such as "I need" / *ho bisogno*, "he needs" / *hai bisogno*, etc. "I like" / *mi piace*, again the same rule applies to *tu* / *lui* / *lei* / *loro* / *noi* / *vostro* in regards to *piace* and *bisogno*. See page 39 to learn more.

21

Place	Luogo/ posto
Easy	Facile
To find	Trovare
To look for / to search	Cercare
Near / Close	Vicino / vicina
To wait	Aspettare
To sell	Vendere
To use	Utilizzare / usare
To know	Sapere
To decide	Decidere
That (*conjunction*)	Che
Two	Due
To	A

This place is easy to find
Questo luogo è facile da trovare
I need to look for you next to the car
Ho bisogno di cercarti vicino alla macchina
I am saying to wait until tomorrow
Sto dicendo di aspettare fino a domani
It's easy to sell this table
E 'facile vendere questo tavolo
I want to use this
Voglio usare questo
I need to know where is the house
Ho bisogno di sapere dove si trova la casa
I need to decide between both places
Ho bisogno di decidere tra due luoghi
I need to know that everything is ok
Ho bisogno di sapere che tutto è ok

*In Italian, "I am" has two definitions: *sono* and *sto*. Usually *sono* refers to a more permanent sense. For example, *sono italiano* / "I am Italian" and *sono un uomo* / "I am a man," while *sto* is more of a temporary case. For example, *sto bene* and *sto* male. *Sto* is also used to indicate movement and locations. Although, similar to every language, there are exceptions to the rule such as *sono stanco* / "I am tired." Some of these irregular cases may need to be memorized. Again, this isn't a grammar book.

*This *isn't* a phrase book! The purpose of this book is *solely* to provide you with the tools to create *your own* sentences!

Because	Perché
To buy	Comprare
Both	Entrambi
Them | They	(M) Essi (F) Esse / (M) Loro (F) Loro
Their	La loro
Book / books	Libro / libri
Mine	Mio / mia
To understand	Capire
Problem / Problems	Problema / problemi
I do / I am doing	Faccio / sto facendo
Like this	Così
To look	Guardare
Myself	Io
Each / every	Ogni
Food	Cibo
Water	Acqua
Hotel	Hotel

I like this hotel because I want to look at the beach
Mi piace quest'hotel perché voglio guardare la spiaggia
I want to buy a bottle of water
Voglio comprare una bottiglia d'acqua
I do it like this each day
Io faccio questo così ogni giorno
Both of them have enough food
Entrambi hanno cibo a sufficienza
This is the book, and this book is mine
Questo è il libro, e questo libro è mio
I need to understand the problem
Ho bisogno di capire il problema
From the hotel I have a view of the city
Dall'hotel ho una vista della città
I can work today
Posso lavorare oggi
I do my homework
Faccio i miei compiti

*In Italian, male nouns end in o; usually their plural form ends with an *i*. Female nouns end in *a*; usually their plural form ends with an *e*. For example, "boy" / *ragazzo*, "boys" / *ragazzi*, "girl" / *ragazza*, "girls" / *ragazze*. Female nouns that end in ea, when pluralized, become *ee*. Female nouns ending in *ca*, their plural form ends in *che*. Nouns ending with an e usually will end with an i when pluralized. Words of foreign origin when pluralized will stay the same, for example, "the motel" / *il motel* and "the motels" / *i motel*.

I like	Mi piace
There is / There are	C'è / ci sono
Family / Parents	Famiglia / Genitori
Why	Perché
To say	Dire
Something	Qualcosa
To go	Andare
Ready	Pronto
Soon	Presto
To work	Lavorare
Who	Chi
To stay	Stare

I like to stay at my house with my parents
Mi piace stare a casa mia con miei genitori
I want to know why?
Voglio sapere perché
Do I need to say something important?
Ho bisogno dire qualcosa importante?
I am there with him
sono là con lui
I am busy, but I need to be ready soon
Io sono impegnato, ma ho bisogno di essere pronto presto
I like to go to work
Mi piace andare a lavorare
Who is there?
Chi è là?
I want to know if they are here, because I want to go outside
Voglio sapere se sono qui, perché voglio andare fuori
There are seven dolls
Ci sono sette bambole

*In Italian, "I need" is *ho bisogno,* and "do I need" is *ho bisogno* as well. Please see page 39 to learn more.

*In Italian, the verb like / *piace* changes to *piacciono* whenever the noun is pluralized. For example, "I like the house" is *mi piace la casa.* However, "I like the houses" is mi *piacciono le case.* The same rule applies to other possessive adjectives as well: *ti piacciono, le piacciono, gli piacciono, vi piacciono,* and *piacciono a loro.*

How much	Quanto
To bring	Portare
With me	Con mei
Instead	Invece
Only	Solo / soltano
When	Quando
I can / Can I?	Posso / posso?
Or	O
Were	Erano
Without me	Senza me
Fast	Veloce
Slow	Lento, lentamente, piano
Cold	Freddo
Inside	Interno
To eat	Mangiare
Hot	Caldo
To Drive	Guidare

How much money do I need to bring with me?
Quanti soldi devo portare con me?
Instead of this cake, I like that cake
Invece di questa torta mi piace quella torta
Only when you can
Solo quando tu puoi
They were without me yesterday
Erano senza di me ieri
I need to drive the car very fast or very slowly
Ho bisogno di guidare la macchina molto veloce o molto lentamente
It is cold inside the library
Fa freddo all'interno della libreria
Yes, I like to eat this hot for my lunch
Sì, mi piace mangiare questa calda per il mio pranzo

To answer	Rispondere
To fly	Volare
I must	Devo
To travel	Viaggiare
To learn	Imparare
How	Come
To swim	Nuotare
To practice	Practicare
To play	Giocare
To leave	Lasciare
Many/much /a lot	(M)Molto (F)Molta
I go to	Vado a
First	Prima
Time / Times	Volta / volte

I need to answer many questions
Ho bisogno di rispondere a molte domande
The bird must fly
L'uccello deve volare
I need to learn to swim at the pool
Ho bisogno di imparare nuotare in piscina
I want to learn everything about how to play better tennis
Voglio imparare tutto su come giocare meglio a tennis
I want to leave this here for you when I go to travel the world
Voglio lasciare questo qui per te quando vado a viaggiare per il mondo
Since the first time
Dalla prima volta
The children are yours
I bambini sono tuoi

*In Italian, "many," "much," and "a lot" is *molto* (m), *molti* (m. plur.), *molta* (f), and *molte* (f. plur.).
*With the knowledge you've gained so far, now try to create your own sentences!

Nobody / Anyone	Nessuno /chiunque
Against	Contro
Us	Noi
To visit	Visitare
Mom / Mother	Mamma
To give	Dare
Which	Quale
To meet	Incontrare
Someone	Qualcuno
Just	Soltanto
To walk	Camminare
Around	Intorno
Towards	Verso
Than	Che / di
Nothing	Niente

Something is better than nothing
Qualcosa è meglio di niente
I am against him
Io sono contro di lui
We go to visit my family each week
Andiamo a visitare la mia famiglia ogni settimana
I need to give you something
Ho bisogno darti qualcosa
Do you want to meet someone
Vuoi incontrare qualcuno?
I am here on Wednesdays as well
Sono qui anche il mercoledì
You do this everyday?
Tu fai questo tutti i giorni?

*In Italian the pronoun "you" has three different definitions: *tu, ti,* and *te.*
Tu is the subject pronoun "you" (informal), for example, *tu vuoi* / "do you want."
Ti is an object pronoun, for example, *ti mostro come* / "I show you how." In Italian, we use *ti* when someone is doing something "to you" or "at you." *Ti* is a direct and indirect object pronoun, the person who is actually affected by the action that is being carried out. But the *ti* comes before the conjugated verb. For example, "I send you" is *ti mando* and "I permit you" is ti *permetto.* In the event the verb is in the infinitive form, the ti follows the verb and connects to the end as a suffix, and you must also remove the e at the end of that verb:
- "to give" / *dare*
- "to give you" / *darti*
Te is used after a verb (*ho bisogno te* / "I need you") as a prepositional pronoun, meaning it goes with a preposition (like *per te*).

I have	Ho
Don't	Non
Friend	(**Male**)Amico /(**female**)amica
To borrow	Prendere in prestito
To look like	Apparire
Grandfather	Nonno
To want	Volere
Wrong / incorrect	Scorretto
To continue	Continuare
Way	(*path*)Via / (*method*) maniera
That's why	Quindi
To show	Mostrare
To prepare	Preparare
I am not going	Non vado

Do you want to look like Arnold?
Vuoi apparire come Arnold?
I want to borrow this book for my grandfather
Voglio prendere in prestito questo libro per mio nonno
I want to drive and to continue on this way to my house
Voglio guidare e continuare per questa via a casa mia
I have a friend, that's why I want to stay in Rome
Ho un amico, per questo voglio stare a Roma
I am not going to see anyone here
Non vedo nessuno qui
I need to show you how to prepare breakfast
Ho bisogno di mostrarti come preparare la colazione
Why don't you have the book?
Perché non hai il libro?
That is incorrect, I don't need the car today
Questo è scorretto, non ho bisogno la macchina oggi

To remember	Ricordare
About (*on*)	Su
About (*proximity*)	Circa
Number	Numero
Hour	Ora
Dark / darkness	Scuro / oscurità
Grandmother	Nonna
Five	Cinque
Minute / Minutes	Minuto / Minuti
More	Più
To think	Pensare
To do	Fare
To come	Venire
To hear	Sentire
Last	(M)Ultimo /(F)Ultima

You must remember my number
Tu devi ricordare il mio numero
This is the last hour of darkness
Questa è l'ultima ora delle sera
I want to come and to hear my grandmother speak Italian today
Voglio venire e sentire la mia nonna parlare oggi italiano
I need to think more about this, and what to do
Ho bisogno di pensare di più su questo, e di che cosa fare
From here until there, it's only five minutes
Da qui fino a lì, è a soli cinque minuti

We	Noi
To leave (*a place*)	Andare
To leave (*something*)	Lasciare
Again	Ancora
Italy	Italia
To take	Prendere
To try	Provare
To rent	Affittare
Without her	Senza lei
We are	Siamo
To turn off	Spegnere
To ask	Chiedere
To stop	Fermare
Permission	Permesso / autorizzazione

He needs to leave and rent a house at the beach
Ha bisogno di andare e affittare una casa al mare
I want to pass the test without her
Voglio passare il test senza di lei
We are here a long time
Siamo qui da molto tempo
I need to turn off the lights early tonight
Ho bisogno spegnere le luci presto stasera
We want to stop here
Noi vogliamo fermarci qui
We came from Sicily
Siamo venuti dalla Sicilia
The same building
Lo stesso edificio
I want to ask permission to go
Voglio chiedere il permesso di andare

*In Italian, *molto* can mean "very" and it can mean "long."

To open	Aprire
To buy	Comprare
To pay	Pagare
On	Su
Without	Senza
Sister	Sorella
To hope	Sperare
To live	Vivere
Nice to meet you	Piacere di conoscerti
Name	Nome
Last name	Cognome
To return	Tornare
Our	Nostro
Door	Porta

I need to open the door for my sister
Ho bisogno di aprire la porta per mia sorella
I need to buy something
Ho bisogno di comprare qualche cosa
I want to meet your sisters
Voglio conoscere le tue sorelle
Nice to meet you, what is your name and your last name?
Piacere di conoscerti, come ti chiami e il tuo cognome?
(Formal) Piacere di conoscerla, come si chiami e il suo cognome?
To hope for the better in the future
Sperare il meglio per il futuro
I want to return from the United States and to live without problems in Italy
Voglio tornare dagli Stati Uniti e vivere in Italia senza avere problemi
Why are you sad right now?
Perche' sei triste adesso?
This is our house on the hill
Questa e la nostra casa sulla colina

*When the preposition "on" is followed by the article "the," they form a suffix:
- on the hill / *sua + la colina = sulla colina*.
Depending on each case, the suffix changes:
- *su + il = sul, su + lo = su*
- *su + la = sulla, su + i = sui*
- *su + gli = sugli, su + le = sulle*
Avere means "to have."

To happen	Accadere
To order	Ordinare
To drink	Bere
Excuse me	Scusi
Child	(M)Bambino/ (F)bambina
Woman	Donna
To begin / To start	Iniziare
To finish	Finire
To help	Aiutare
To smoke	Fumare
To love	Amare
To talk / To Speak	Parlare

This must happen today

Questo deve accadere oggi

Excuse me, my child is here as well

Scusami, il mio bambino è anche qui

I love you

Ti amo

I see you

Ti vedo

I need you

Ho bisogno di te

I need to begin soon to be able to finish at 3 o'clock in the afternoon

Ho bisogno di iniziare presto per essere in grado di finire alle 3 del pomeriggio

I want to help

Voglio aiutare

I don't want to smoke again

Non voglio fumare di nuovo

I want to learn to speak Italian

Voglio imparare a parlare italiano

*In Italian, the possessive adjectives are always preceded by the article "the."
- *"my"—il mio, la mia, i miei, le mie*
- *"his" and "her"—il suo, la sua, i suoi, le sue*
The same rule applies to other possessive adjectives as well.
*In Italian, there are two cases for the verb "can" / "to be able to." *Posso* is the first person conjugated form of the infinitive verb potere, which means "being allowed" to do something. "Can I go?" / *posso andare? Grado* is the first person conjugated form of the infinitive verb *riuscire,* which means "to succeed." "I can" / "am able to do this" / *io sono in grado di fare questo.*

To read	Leggere
To write	Scrivere
To teach	Insegnare
To close	Chiudere
To turn on	Accendere
To prefer	Preferire
To put	Mettere
Less	Meno
Sun	Sole
Month / months	Mese / messi
I Talk	Parlo
Exact	Esatto
To choose	Scegliere

I need this book to learn how to read and write in Italian because I want to teach in Italy
Ho bisogno di questo libro per imparare a leggere e scrivere in Italiano perché voglio insegnare in Italia
I want to close the door of the house and not to turn on the light
Voglio chiudere la porta della casa e non accendere la luce
I prefer to put the gift here
Io preferisco mettere il regalo qui
I want to pay less than you for the dinner
Io voglio pagare meno che tu per la cena
I speak with the boy and the girl in Italian
Parlo con il ragazzo e la ragazza in italiano
There is sun outside today
C'è sole fuori oggi
Is it possible to know the exact date?
E' possibile sapere la data esatta?
I need to go to sleep now in order to wake up early so I can take a taxi to the airport
Ho bisogno di dormirme ora, per svegliarme prima per prendere un taxi al'aeroporto.

*With the knowledge you've gained so far, now try to create your own sentences!

To exchange	Scambiare
To call	Chiamare
Brother	Fratello
Dad	Papà
To sit	Sedersi
Together	Insieme
To change	Cambiare
Of course	Certo
Welcome	Benvenuto
During	Durante
Years	Anno/anni
Sky	Cielo
Up	Su
Down	Giù
Sorry	Dispiace
To follow	Seguire
Her	Lei
Big	Grande
New	Nuovo
Never	Mai

I don't want to exchange this money at the bank
Non voglio scambiare il denaro in banca
I want to call my brother and my dad today
Voglio chiamare mio fratello e mio padre oggi
Of course I can come to the theater, and I want to sit together with you and with your sister
Certo posso venire a teatro, e voglio sedermi insieme con te e con tua sorella
I need to go down to see your new house
Ho bisogno di andare giù per vedere la vostra nuova casa
I can see the sky from the window
Posso vedere il cielo dalla finestra
I am sorry, but he wants to follow her to the store
Mi dispiace, ma vuole seguirla al negozio
It never rains
Non piova mai

To allow	Consentire
To believe	Credere
Morning	Mattina
Except	Tranne
To promise	Promettere
Good night	Buona notte
To recognize	Riconoscere
People	Gente
To move	Spostare
Far	Lontano
Different	Differente / diverso
Man	Uomo
To enter	Entrare
To receive	Ricevere
Throughout	Durante
Good afternoon	Buon pomeriggio
Through	Attraverso
Him / Her	Lui / lei

I need to allow him to go with us, he is a different man now
Ho bisogno di permettergli di andare con noi, lui è un uomo diverso ora
I believe everything, except for this
Credo tutto, tranne questo
I must promise to say good night to my parents each night
Devo promettere di dire la buona notte ai miei genitori ogni notte
They need to recognize the people from Italy very quickly
Hanno bisogno di riconoscere le persone dall'Italia molto velocemente
I need to move your cat to another chair
Ho bisogno di spostare il vostro gatto a un'altra sedia
They want to enter the competition and receive a free book
Vogliono partecipare al concorso e ricevere un libro gratuito
I see the sun throughout the morning from the kitchen
Vedo il sole durante la mattina dalla cucina
I go into the house but not through the yard
Vado in casa, ma non attraverso il cortile

---

*In Italian we use *a* to indicate "to". However the plural case of "to" is *ai*.

To wish	Augurare
Bad	Cattivo
To Get	Ottenere
To forget	Dimenticare
Everybody / Everyone	Tutti
Although	Anche se
To feel	Sentire
Great	Grande
Next	Prossimo
To like	Piacere
In front	Di fronte
Person	Dietro
Behind	Persona
Well	Bene
Goodbye	Arrivederci
Restaurant	Ristorante
Bathroom	Bagno

I don't want to wish you anything bad
Non voglio augurarti nulla di male
I must forget everybody from my past in order to feel well
Devo dimenticarmi di tutti dal mio passato per sentirmi bene
I am next to the person behind you
Sono accanto alla persona dietro di te
There is a great person in front of me
C'e una bella persona di fronte a me
I say goodbye to my friends
Dico arrivederci ai mie amici
In which part of the restaurant is the bathroom?
In quale parte del ristorante e' il bagno?
She has to get a car before the next year
Lei deve prendere una automobile prima del prossimo anno
I want to like the house, but it is very small
Voglio che la casa mi piaccia, ma e' molto piccola

To remove	Rimuovere
Please	Per favore
Beautiful	Bello / bella
To lift	Sollevare
Include / Including	Compreso
Belong	Appartenere
To hold	Tenere
To check	Verificare
Small	Piccolo
Real	Vero
Week	Settimana
Size	Misura
Even though	Anche se
Doesn't	Non
So	Così (*thus*) / tanto (*so much*)
Price	Prezzo

She wants to remove this door please
Vuole rimuovere questa porta per favore
This doesn't belong here, I need to check again
Questo non appartiene qui, ho bisogno di verificare di nuovo
This week the weather was very beautiful
Questa settimana il tempo era molto bello
I need to know which is the real diamond
Ho bisogno di sapere qual'è il vero diamante
We need to check the size of the house
Abbiamo bisogno di controllare la dimensione della casa
I want to lift this, that's why you need to hold it high
Voglio alzare questo, quindi è necessario tenerlo alto
I can pay this although that the price is expensive
Posso pagare questo, anche se il prezzo è caro
Including everything is this price correct?
Tutto incluso è il prezzo corretto?

BUILDING BRIDGES

In Building Bridges, we take six conjugated verbs that have been selected after studies I have conducted for several months in order to determine which verbs are most commonly conjugated, and which are then automatically followed by an infinitive verb. For example, once you know how to say, "I need," "I want," "I can," and "I like," you will be able to connect words and say almost anything you want more correctly and understandably. The following three pages contain these six conjugated verbs in first, second, third, fourth, and fifth person, as well as some sample sentences. Please master the entire program up until here prior to venturing onto this section.

I want	Voglio
I need	Ho bisogno
I can	Posso
I like	Mi piace
I go	Vado
I have to /I must	Devo

I want to go to my house
Voglio andare a casa mia
I can go with you to the bus station
Posso venire con te alla stazione degli autobus
I need to walk to the museum
Ho bisogno di camminare al museo
I like to take the train
Mi piace prendere il treno
I have to speak to my teacher
Devo parlare con il mio insegnante

Please master pages 16-38, prior to attempting the following two pages!!

You want / do you want? - Vuoi / vuoi?
He wants / does he want? - Vuole / vuole?
She wants / does she want? - Vuole / vuole?
We want / do we want? - Vogliamo / vogliamo?
They want / do they want? - Vogliono / vogliono?
You (plural/ formal sing) - Voi volete / voi volete?

You need / do you need? - Hai bisogno / hai bisogno?
He needs / does he need? - Ha bisogno/ ha bisogno?
She needs / does she need? - Ha bisogno / ha bisogno?
We need / do we need? - Abbiamo bisogno / abbiamo bisogno?
They need / do they need? - Hanno bisogno / cosa hanno bisogno?
You (plural/ formal sing) - Voi avete bisogno / voi avete bisogno?

You can / can you? - Puoi / puoi?
He can / can he? - Può / può?
She can / can she? - Può / può?
We can / can we? - Possiamo / possiamo?
They can / can they? - Possono / possono?
You (plural/ formal sing) - Potete/ potete?

You like / do you like? - Ti piace / ti piace ?
He likes / does he like? - Lui piace / lui piace?
She like / does she like? - Lei piace / lei piace?
We like / do we like? - Noi piace / noi piace?
They like / do they like? - A loro piace / a loro piace?
You (plural/ formal sing) - Vi piace / vi piace?

You go / do you go? - Va / vai?
He goes / does he go? - Va / va?
She goes / does she go? - Va / va?
We go / do we go? - Andiamo / andiamo?
They go / do they go? - Vanno / vanno?
You (plural/ formal sing) - Vanno / vanno?

You have / do you have? - Hai / hai?
He has / does he have? - Ha / ha?
She has / does she have? - Ha / ha?
We have / do we have? - Abbiamo / abbiamo?
They have / do they have? - Hanno / hanno?
You (plural/ formal sing) - Hanno / hanno?

You must /must you? - Devi / devi?
He must /must he? - Deve / deve?
She must / must she? - Deve / deve?
We must /must we? - Dobbiamo / dobbiamo?
They must /must they? - Devono / devono?
You (plural) - Devono / devono?

Please master pages 16-38,
prior to attempting this pages!!

Do you want to go?
Vuoi andare?
Does he want to fly?
Vuole volare?
We want to swim
Vogliamo nuotare
Do they want to run?
Vogliono correre?
Do you need to clean?
Hai bisogno di pulire?
She needs to sing a song
Ha bisogno di cantare una canzone
We need to travel
Abbiamo bisogno di viaggiare
They don't need to fight
Non hanno bisogno di lottare
You (plural) need to see
Hanno bisogno di vedere
Can you hear me?
Puoi sentirmi?
Yes, he can dance very well
Si, può ballare molto bene
We can go out tonight
Possiamo uscire stasera
They can break the wood
Loro possono rompere il legno
Do you like to eat here?
Ti piace mangiare qui?

He likes to spend time here
A lui piace trascorrere del tempo qui
We like to fix the house
A noi piace sistemare la casa
They like to cook
A loro piace cucinare
You (plural) like my house
A loro piace la mia casa
Do you go to school today?
Vai a scuola oggi?
He goes fishing
Lui va a pescare
We are going to relax
Stiamo andando a rilassarsi
They go to watch a film
Vanno a guardare un film
Do you have money?
Hai soldi?
She must look outside
Lei deve guardare fuori
We have to sign our names
Dobbiamo firmare i nostri nomi
They have to send the letter
Devono inviare la lettera
You (plural) have to order
Devono ordinare

Other Useful Tools in Italian

Days of the Week

Sunday	Domenica
Monday	Lunedi
Tuesday	Martedì
Wednesday	Mercoledì
Thursday	Giovedi
Friday	Venerdì
Saturday	Sabato

Seasons

Spring	Primavera
Summer	Estate
Autumn	Autunno
Winter	Inverno

Colors

Black	Nero
White	Bianco
Gray	Grigio
Red	Rosso
Blue	Blu
Yellow	Giallo
Green	Verde
Orange	Arancione
Purple	Viola
Brown	Marrone

Numbers

One	Uno
Two	Due
Three	Tre
Four	Quattro
Five	Cinque
Six	Sei
Seven	Sette
Eight	Otto
Nine	Nove
Ten	Dieci

Cardinal Directions

North	Nord
South	Sud
East	Est
West	Ovest

CONGRATULATIONS, NOW YOU ARE ON YOUR OWN!

If you merely absorb the required three hundred and fifty words in this book, you will then have acquired the basis to become conversational in Italian! After memorizing these three hundred and fifty words, this conversational foundational basis that you have just gained will trigger your ability to make improvements in conversational fluency at an amazing speed! However, in order to engage in quick and easy conversational communication, you need a special type of basics, and this book will provide you with just that.

Unlike the foreign language learning systems presently used in schools and universities, along with books and programs that are available on the market today, that focus on everything but being conversational, this method's sole focus is on becoming conversational in Italian as well as any other language. Once you have successfully mastered the required words in this book, there are two techniques that if combined with these essential words, can further enhance your skills and will result in you improving your proficiency tenfold. *However*, these two techniques will only succeed *if* you have completely and successfully absorbed the three hundred and fifty words. *After* you establish the basis for fluent communications by memorizing these words, you can enhance your conversational abilities even more if you use the following two techniques.

The first step is to attend an Italian language class that will enable you to sharpen your grammar. You will gain additional vocabulary and learn past and present tenses, and if you apply these skills that you learn in the class, together with the three hundred and fifty words that you have previously memorized, you will be improving your conversational skills tenfold. You will notice that, conversationally, you will succeed at a much higher rate than any of your classmates. A simple second technique is to choose Italian subtitles while watching a movie. If you have successfully mastered and grasped these three hundred and fifty words, then the combination of the two —those words along with the subtitles—will aid you considerably in putting all the grammar into perspective, and again, conversationally, you will improve tenfold.

Once you have established a basis of quick and easy conversation in Italian with those words that you just attained, every additional word or grammar rule you pick up from there on will be gravy. And these additional words or grammar rules can be combined with the three hundred and fifty words, enriching your conversational abilities even more. Basically, after the research and studies I've conducted with my method over the years, I came to the conclusion that in order to become conversational, you first must learn the words and then learn the grammar.

The Italian language is compatible with the mirror translation technique. Likewise, with *this* language, you can use this mirror translation technique in order to become conversational, enabling you to communicate even more effortlessly. Mirror translation is the method of translating a phrase or sentence, word for word from English to Italian, by using these imperative words that you have acquired through this program (such as the sentences I used in this book). Latin languages, Middle Eastern languages, and Slavic languages, along with a few others, are also compatible with the mirror translation technique. Though you won't be speaking perfectly proper and precise Italian, you will still be fully understood and, conversation-wise, be able to get by just fine.

CONCLUSION

Congratulations! You have completed all the tools needed to master the Italian language, and I hope that this has been a valuable learning experience. Now you have sufficient communication skills to be confident enough to embark on a visit to Italy, impress your friends, and boost your resume so *good luck.*

This program is available in other languages as well, and it is my fervent hope that my language learning programs will be used for good, enabling people from all corners of the globe and from all cultures and religions to be able to communicate harmoniously. After memorizing the required three hundred and fifty words, please perform a daily five-minute exercise by creating sentences in your head using these words. This simple exercise will help you grasp conversational communications even more effectively. Also, once you memorize the vocabulary on each page, follow it by using a notecard to cover the words you have just memorized and test yourself and follow *that* by going back and using this same notecard technique on the pages you studied during the previous days. This repetition technique will assist you in mastering these words in order to provide you with the tools to create your own sentences.

Every day, use this notecard technique on the words that you have just studied.

Everything in life has a catch. The catch here is just consistency. If you just open the book, and after the first few pages of studying the program, you put it down, then you will not gain anything. However, if you consistently dedicate a half hour daily to studying, as well as reviewing what you have learned from previous days, then you will quickly realize why this method is the most effective technique ever created to become conversational in a foreign language. My technique works! For anyone who doubts this technique, all I can say is that it has worked for me and hundreds of others.

Note from the Author

Thank you for your interest in my work. I encourage you to share your overall experience of this book by posting a review. Your review can make a difference! Please feel free to describe how you benefited from my method or provide creative feedback on how I can improve this program. I am constantly seeking ways to enhance the quality of this product, based on personal testimonials and suggestions from individuals like you.

Thanks and best of luck,

Yatir Nitzany